When the Cat Speaks ...
Listen

A purr-fectly good way to enjoy life

Thoughts and Ideas
by Myron

Wendy VanHatten

First Printing, Nov 2011

Published by
Wendy VanHatten Publishing

©2011, Wendy VanHatten

All rights reserved. No part of this publication may be reproduced, stored in a retrieval system, or transmitted in any manner or by any means including but not limited to electronic, mechanical, recorded, or otherwise without the written permission of the author.

Printed in the United States of America

Aris MacInnes
Cover illustration
LiteratiCreative

www.LiteratiCreative.com

Wendy VanHatten
Photographs

www.VHWritingServices.com

Ginger Marks
Design & layout
DocUmeant Designs

www.DocUmeantDesigns.com

ISBN13 978-0-9846627-0-8
ISBN10 0984662707

Words of Praise

"This wonderful book of life lessons reminds me to be nicer to my imaginary friends and makes me wish I had nine lives. It teaches us that we all have a meow deep inside, waiting to come out."—**Franny V**

"As Myron's original human provider, I can say without doubt that he is the brightest as well as the dimmest feline I have ever met. He is truly a savant, the 'Rain Man' of cats. In some ways, Myron is as great a teacher as Yoda. This quote could have come from either of them: 'Much to learn, you still have.'"—**Jim VH**

Dedication

I dedicate this book to all of you who believe life is more enjoyable if you have a good attitude.

After all ... cats and attitude go together.

Myron

Contents

Words of Praise iii

Dedication v

Acknowledgements xi

Chapter One
The Cat Speaks... 1

Chapter Two
Naps are Important 3

Chapter Three
When You Play ... Play Hard 5

Chapter Four
Meow Until You Get Your Way 7

Chapter Five
Don't Waste Sunshine 9

Chapter Six
Hairballs Are Necessary 11

Chapter Seven
Demand Attention 13

Chapter Eight
**Friends Are Important, Even
Imaginary Ones** 15

Chapter Nine
Enjoy Life 17

Chapter Ten
It's Okay to Ignore People 19

Chapter Eleven
Attack When They're Not Looking 21

Chapter Twelve
Grooming Is Essential 23

Chapter Thirteen
Curiosity ... Curiosity ... Curiosity 25

Chapter Fourteen
**Inspect Everything ... AND Always
Keep One Eye Open** 27

Chapter Fifteen
Look Innocent **31**

Chapter Sixteen
A Job Well Done Deserves a Reward **33**

Bonus Section
ABCs According to Myron **37**

Acknowledgements

Thanks from me, a very special cat, to my human family, starting with my first owner Jim. Thanks, Jim, for handing me over to my current owners when you went to Iraq. They were easy to train and treat me like the royalty I am.

Thanks from me also to all those who give me joy in this life.

Myron

Thanks to Myron from me, the writer, for giving such pleasure and enjoyment. Life without a cat ... especially one with such a personality ... is unimaginable.

Thanks also to my dear friend, Julie, who helped edit this and most of all ... kept me on track.

Wendy

"Of all God's creatures, there is only one that cannot be made slave of the lash. That one is the cat. If man could be crossed with the cat it would improve the man, but it would deteriorate the cat."—Mark Twain

Chapter One

The Cat Speaks...

Want to know a secret?

Having nine lives is the **only** way to live. I should know ... I'm a cat. Not just any cat, mind you. I'm special and I know it.

Do you want to be special, too? Then listen to what I have to say, follow my advice, and stick with me.

Here's another secret.

Watch ... Wait ... Pounce. That's the way to go through life. Why?

Watch ... learn how others do things. Wait ... let things come to you. Pounce ... grab whatever it is you need.

If you ask me, kittens now days use up some of their lives too quickly. They just need to learn how to watch, wait, and then pounce. None of this ready ... fire ... aim stuff. But they are like some of you ... they just don't know how to slow down. Then again ... I do remember being a kitten.

Let me introduce myself. My name is Myron. I am an expert in the field of living each day to its fullest and I

Chapter One

want to share my thoughts with you. Are you ready to listen? Sit back, let my wisdom sink in, and enjoy the ride.

But ... before we move on, I need to thank my Ghostwriter. She also serves as my *staff* and is pretty good at making sure all my needs are met.

Hopefully she spelled everything correctly ... especially my name. You see I really needed a Ghostwriter. Since I have no thumbs it makes it kind of hard to type.

Enjoy...

Myron

Chapter Two

Naps are Important

My philosophy is this. Nap 16 of every 24 hours. This is the first crucial step to living your life to the fullest. Some of my favorite nap times happen after I watch birds in the morning, or after I've finished eating, or maybe after bathing, or possibly after chasing a mouse (toy one, of course), or definitely after being groomed, and always after I wake up.

If I see a lap, it's naptime. A basket of clean laundry begs for me to nap. Hide on a chair under the dining room table, curl up on a new rug (or an old one), squeeze into an open

Chapter Two

drawer, or find the darkest corner in the closet. Hop up on the back of the sofa ... and relax. Summertime is a good time for a nap. So are winter, spring, and fall. For that matter morning, afternoon, evening, and night time is nap time.

Naps are meant to be enjoyed and we cats do a great job of that. Why do you think they call them "cat naps?" No one ever heard of "dog naps."

It doesn't matter whether the nap is ten minutes or an hour. And as long as you are comfortable it really doesn't matter where you take your nap.

Nothing is more peaceful than seeing a cat take a nap. Right?

Want to know how to get the most out of your life? Nap ... early and often. That's my motto.

Chapter Three

When You Play ... Play Hard

We've all been told that to maintain a healthy life, everybody needs aerobic exercise. For that matter, you are supposed to engage in good exercises to get your blood flowing and keep your heart rate up. Most of you think of jogging or walking, swimming or tennis, lifting weights or cycling.

I say ... forget those.

Chapter Three

Here's a better idea. Try pouncing, attacking, stalking, hiding, wiggling, chasing, or batting. Use all your muscles and get a total body workout. Or if you prefer, only exercise your back feet. It doesn't matter. It's all exercise and it works however you do it.

How do I find time? Easy. Whenever the mood strikes ... I play. Actually, whenever something moves that gets my attention ... I play.

Manage to work in some play time every day and you'll never have to worry about exercising again. For me, I attack my sister, toys, rubber bands, bugs, pens on the counter, rugs, the air, my food, the shower curtain, invisible friends ... my list goes on and on. There is no limit to *my toys*. In fact, the world is my toy box.

Now get up off the couch and go chase something.

Chapter Four

Meow Until You Get Your Way

Maybe this won't work for you, but it does wonders for what I want in life. I meow until I get my way.

Depending upon my mood I can ask, complain, scold, demand, or beg. Listen closely. Do you hear me talking in just one sentence or in complete paragraphs? Do I sound annoyed with you? Am I trying to tell you my food bowl is empty or the ice disappeared from my water bowl? Is the house on fire or am I out of treats?

Is someone coming to the door or do I want attention ... now? If you are spending too much time not paying attention to me ... I'll meow until you stop what you're doing and pet me.

Maybe I'm in a cute mood and want to snuggle with you. I'll meow to let you know it. Perhaps it's midnight and I just feel like meowing in the dark. It sure is fun to listen to that meow echo down the hall. Try it sometime.

Chapter Four

Practice your meows until you have one you can use for every situation. I don't just have one meow, you know. Pay attention, please.

Work on it ... I know you have a meow deep inside of you somewhere.

Chapter Five

Don't Waste Sunshine

Ahh ... sunshine. One of the simple pleasures of life.

If you can't find me, look for the sunniest room in the house. I've perfected the art of total relaxation ... a cat soaking up the sun. If you ask me, I think cats are the original sun worshippers. Maybe that's why cats were so revered in Egypt. It's sunny there, right?

There's one important thing you need to know about snoozing in the sun. When you're finished you need to

Chapter Five

stretch out every kink from your paws to your tail. Doesn't matter how many times a day you catch some sun. This is the rule. First you snooze ... then you stretch.

Now, you may have to move around the house to find the best sun. It plays tricks on you and moves from window to window. In reality you could say I was exercising in between naps in the sun. Come to think of it, this is an exercise routine I can live with.

And nothing rejuvenates you like a good nap in the sun. If you ask me, sunshine is good for the soul.

Chapter Six

Hairballs Are Necessary

Okay, this is not pleasant. But it is part of life. Believe me, nothing sounds worse than a cat coughing up a hairball.

Nothing.

I should know. It sounds painful and just plain icky. And sometimes it is. But if you're a cat, it's a way of life. You groom me, comb me, and I still shed. So, when I clean myself with my tongue the hair has to go somewhere. Hence, a hairball.

What do hairballs have to do with life?

Well ... as for many things in life, you deal with unpleasant situations. Cough 'em up and move on.

Enough on that ...

Chapter Seven

Demand Attention

Let's start by saying *all demands are not bad*. Let's also say *demanding attention is an art*. And no one is better at demanding attention than us cats.

Your job is to know what I mean. When I tilt my head and give you a quizzical look ... it means I wonder if you know what you're doing. Did you really just paint that wall fire engine red? Can't you see it clashes with the pink sofa?

A haughty stare from me is reserved for special occasions. This is when you really have no idea what you're doing.

Chapter Seven

Day old food in my dish? Come on ... In fact, I'd roll my eyes if I could.

Swishing my tail usually implies I'm disgusted with you. Can't you see I'm finished with the brushing and combing routine? Move out of my way.

If I rub my head on your face or give you a little head nudge ... I really do want some undivided attention. And I want it now. I love swiping at your pen and hope it jumps out of your hand and onto the floor. I was bored anyway and needed something to chase. When I nip at your fingers as they move across the keyboard it's only because they're in my space.

I could go on, but you really only need to know the basic ones.

Keep in mind; demands do not have to be logical. Maybe I'm telling you that my food bowl is empty right now ... or maybe it will be empty in the next day or so. You see, there is nothing logical about the demand or the timing of that demand.

Ignore my demands, though, and be prepared for the consequences. Perhaps you will get an "I can't believe I put up with you" glare as I wander off to more important activities.

No point in wasting too much time. Life is too short to dwell on unmet demands.

Chapter Eight

Friends Are Important, Even Imaginary Ones

In case you're wondering, my world is full of friends. Of course there is my sister, if you count her as a friend. Then there are the birds chirping and flitting about outside the window, neighborhood cats wandering across the street, an occasional dog that visits my front door ... and all my imaginary friends.

I'm never alone.

My imaginary friends are special. They share secrets with me. I never have to wonder if someone will play with me. For instance, the game of tag has limitless players as my friends chase me and I chase them. One can sneak up behind me, tap me on the shoulder, and I'm off at mach 10 trying to catch him.

Plus my friends are inventive. They jump up on the counter and find pens for us to chase. Zooming down the hall, skidding around the corner, and disappearing under the chair is just part of the game. I must find them. Of course, they have been known to knock over a lamp in their haste to get away from me.

Chapter Eight

But really ... who put that lamp there anyway? Such is life.

Don't you see ... friends make life so nice?

Chapter Nine

Enjoy Life

Maybe I don't have to worry about such mundane things as jobs, paychecks, grocery shopping, mowing the lawn, or cleaning the house. I know I enjoy my pampered life. And that's okay. Did I mention I'm a cat? Being pampered is my way of life.

After all, my food dish is always full, my litter box is always cleaned, and the simple necessities of comfort are taken care of for me. "Hang loose" is my motto most days. Heck, I don't even know about daily stress or depression.

Chapter Nine

Life is good. However, I do more than *just* eat, lie around, and enjoy life. Did you know that cats have that sixth sense allowing them to perceive things? Well ... we do.

You may think I'm not paying attention. You would be wrong. I know when you've had a bad day, or when you need a hug, or when I should purr in your face. That's my job.

I enjoy life so much, especially when I pay attention to my best friend ... you.

Chapter Ten

It's Okay to Ignore People

Cats are good at this. We are the original "I'll take a message and get back to you ... when I'm ready."

You can call, coax, plead, or bribe. But if I'm not ready ... you really don't exist. I may look at you ... I may not. And just because my ears twitch, it doesn't mean I'm at your beck and call.

Part of the mystery surrounding us is our ability to ignore someone one minute and be their best friend the next.

If you are paying attention, the signs you are about to be ignored are obvious. We don't stomp our feet, shout, swear, or point fingers. A look of dismissal or well timed exit from the room is all it takes.

Congratulations. You have just been ignored in true cat style.

Chapter Eleven

Attack When They're Not Looking

The element of surprise always works for me.

I can sneak up on anyone or anything ... an inanimate object, birds on the patio, unsuspecting toes under the table, empty paper bags, and especially my sister. Now if only my wiggling rear end wouldn't give me away.

Most of the time, I am so quiet you don't even hear me coming. My stealth skills are so good; maybe I should join the Army.

However, at times I have been known to be a *little* louder. Galloping through the house or down the hallway I can pursue anyone who gets in my path. Sometimes my back claws click and scratch on the wood floor. Once in a while I skid around a corner, miss the doorway, and thunk into the side of the door frame. Ouch.

For me, I don't really care what time of day or night it is. If it needs to be attacked ... I'm your cat.

Chapter Eleven

You thought the pretty new flowering plant you brought into the house and put up on a high shelf in the living room was safe? Nope. It looked like a salad to me. And how do you think your new necklace ended up under the bed? You shouldn't have left it in plain site on the dresser. It was just too shiny.

In reality, both were just unsuspecting targets that I snuck up on. They didn't even see me coming.

Chapter Twelve

Grooming Is Essential

Who wants to go through life not properly groomed? Didn't your mother teach you to go out into the world with clean underwear? Whatever that means ...

Every day I clean every inch of my fur. Why do I do this? I'm not sure ... I think I read it had something to do with my ancestors. In the wild a lion, tiger, or leopard had to clean their fur fastidiously before the next hunt. They couldn't surprise the next meal still smelling like the last one.

Now I don't hunt wild game, or tame game for that matter, but I still have the need to be groomed. Like the big cats, it is essential to me as well.

Refer back to the chapter on hairballs if you want to know what comes next.

Chapter Thirteen

Curiosity ... Curiosity ... Curiosity

Okay ... this one is important to an enjoyable life.

As I always say, "If you aren't curious about life, you might as well live under the bed."

I know my curiosity brightens your day and sometimes makes you laugh. I also know my curiosity got me in trouble in a big way more than once.

But ...

Chapter Thirteen

The vase that broke wasn't really my fault. If there hadn't been water in it, I wouldn't have tried to stick my whole head in that vase. Then when it proceeded to fall off the counter; it broke all by itself. Actually I didn't break it ... the floor did.

And the roll of paper towels on the floor. Not sure what happened there. I was just scooting them around and batting at them with my back claws when they started to shred. And they kept shredding and shredding. Pretty soon I couldn't even tell where the floor was. That was a mess.

By the way, the Christmas tree also sheds. It sheds its ornaments. I just try to corral them and put them back under the tree. Somehow I keep getting blamed for knocking them off and chasing them throughout the house. Crazy ornaments.

After all if I'm not supposed to thoroughly check things out, why are they here?

Chapter Fourteen

Inspect Everything ... AND Always Keep One Eye Open

You must keep an eye on what is going on in the house. After all, it is your house.

For instance, suitcases come out at certain times. From my experience they are not your friend. Suitcases can only

Chapter Fourteen

mean one thing ... someone is going away. And probably not taking me.

My advice? Don't just let the suitcases sit there on the bed, gaping open, and empty. Crawl in, look in all the cracks and crevices, move any clothes out of the way, and lie down. Or better yet, take a nap on the clothes. No one is going anywhere with me in the suitcase.

This applies to other interesting pieces brought in to the house as well. Paper bags for instance just beg to be explored and inspected. They make a great noise. Chew a corner off and you can spy on everybody and everything. No one will see you ... trust me.

Shoe boxes ... another item in need of inspection. They don't provide as nice a hiding spot but they do work for a cat nap.

I'll let you in on another little secret. Cats pay attention to everything. I may look like I'm asleep but my ears and eyes are constantly alert.

When you open a new can of food, pick up the treat bag, get my comb out of the basket, or put clean sheets on the bed I am a split second away from participating.

How else do I know it's time to go to the vet? I pay attention. That dreaded cat carrier makes a special noise when it's brought out of its hiding spot. I hear it and it's time to hide ... really hide. The vet does things to me I don't like. Pay attention ... I tell you.

Remember ... life is so much more interesting when you know what's going on.

Chapter Fifteen

Look Innocent

Face it. Cats get blamed for everything.

Everything.

Ever heard of the musical *CATS*? Those poor cats were blamed for taking food, pearls, and winter vests as well as breaking a Ming vase. Whatever that is...

What do I do? I have perfected my *innocent look*. It takes practice but is so worth it, especially with my sister being around. She can take the blame. She's half deaf anyway so...

Here's another secret ... but you can't share it with anybody else.

Just tilt your head sideways ... look down a little ... give whoever you need to a *who me* stare ... raise your eyebrows ever so slightly ... and hold the pose. No one could possibly blame you after that look.

Try it ... you'll love it.

Chapter Sixteen

A Job Well Done Deserves a Reward

In life there are rewards for doing a good job. In my world those rewards are treats.

Watch me. I can come when I'm called, if I think it's important. I will fetch toys, if I'm in the mood. I always look cute, that's a given. I can sit patiently while being combed, if I have nothing better to do.

Or ... better yet I can just be myself. That's the best.

After all, being a cat is what it's all about.

What's your story?

Bonus Section

Everyone learns their ABC's. Mine are special and I'm sharing them with you. I'll bet you enjoy them just as much I do.

Have a purr-fectly great day ...

ABCs According to Myron

Arch your back when you stretch ... it makes you look thinner.

Bask in every sunbeam.

Catch at least ten naps every day.

Dig those claws into whatever is available ... if you don't use 'em, you might lose 'em.

Envy no one.

Fur is meant to share.

Greet each day with a yawn.

Hairballs are just part of living.

Indulge often.

Jump into an available lap.

Bonus Section

Kittens are such pains.

Love your staff ... a.k.a. family.

Make an entrance.

Nine lives are barely enough.

Only the best ... after all I am a cat.

Purrrr loudly ... at every opportunity.

Quiet please ... I'm trying to nap here.

Real cats rule.

Scratch behind my ears ... please.

Thunder through the house chasing imaginary friends ... especially at night.

Unleash your inner lion.

Vary your hiding places ... under the sheets, in a laundry basket, or even on top of a black shirt.

Wander nightly ... even if it's just down the hall.

Xercize ... you must be kidding.

Your bath time is calling.

Zebras might be fun to chase.

www.ingramcontent.com/pod-product-compliance
Lightning Source LLC
Chambersburg PA
CBHW072038060426
42449CB00010BA/2339